Belonging

A Collection of Poems about Love, Loss, and the Search for Meaning

EMMA MATHEWS

Belonging

A Collection of Poems about Love, Loss, and the Search for Meaning

Emma Mathews

Published by:
www.AcheloisBooks.com

ISBN: 978-0-578-76661-4

All proceeds from the sale of this book will be
donated to Ocean Conservancy.

To Mom and Dad, thank you for everything.

CONTENTS

The Bare

The thirst for purpose
Void of motivation.
Divinely ironic
Empty ambition.

For who was she
But the child of the children
Of endurance?
A byproduct of the American Dream?
Generations, clawing their way
Through social ranks and restrictions,
Ending in the composition of a child
Unwilling, or unable, to pour that same
Blood, sweat, tears of success into life.

Perhaps I do not fear opportunity.
Perhaps I fear responsibility
That decades of neglect have forced into our hands,
We are perpetrators of our own destruction.

A century after them and we are Lost too,
Trapped in the unfamiliar wasteland
Of a post-post-war world
Waiting
Counting down to the next one,
The ender of days,
Suffrage of the earth,
Long awaited and easily dismissed.

The face of the new world,
Unraveled, we are bare.

A Worm Fell Out

Paper power in their hands
And cruelty in their veins,
Eager, gnashing teeth,
Let them gape at the ghastly chains!

Gather 'round to watch the show,
Witness the abhorrent,
Travesty of God,
A freak!

Gather 'round 'til you've suckled
Every
Drop of life
From her cracked, disintegrating skin!

Thrice dead and thrice judged,
A pitiful performance!
Die, die again!
Beautifully, like Lady Lazarus,
Or comically, like Miss Baartman.

But alas!
What if a day comes when dried worms
Spill from the empty pockets of her eyes
And the well of green runs dry?

Why, dissect her, of course!
Preserve some pieces for show,
Auction the rest!

She'll meet her God when they're done with her,
When they've stripped the scent of life from her bones
And determined the rest to be worthless.
Profitless.
Yes, she'll meet her God when they say she can.

Beware!

Fie! The dark and wretched night descends,
And with it, the plummeting morality of man!
Devilish creatures in the night,
Beware, beware!
Have you tempted them thus?
Have you lured them from their righteous bonds?
Ensnared them with your open womanhood?

Mourn, mourn!
Until the morn
When virgin blood runs thick!
Beware, beware!
The wicked hearts of men
Prowl as night comes quick!

Fill your lungs with sweet, clean air
For one day they will own it.

High above the guilt they've buried,
Mount Olympus soars and sours,
Home of the gods,
Styx of the soul.

Dig your nails into the dirt,
Feel its motherly embrace
While you can,
It will shrivel and recede,
Summoned by paper,
Replaced by detritus.

The rebirth has failed.
Revolution has given way to destitution,
Now you must bear the weight of our negligence
Upon your crumbling shoulders,
Atlas, my dear.

Drink your fill
Of the unspoiled blood of earth,
For, once they can, they will drain it from your
Hands.

Be afraid, my child,
Their capacity for cruelty is boundless,
They are gilded and guided by gold and glory.

Their greed is immortal,
But their power an illusion.
When the skies turn grey,
Their green will not restore her.
Atlas will rise.

Remember to hold yourself close,
They will try to buy you too.

Angel of Mundanity

Down,
Down the drain,
Down the deep, dark, dank dungeon.
Dreary, is it not?
Disgusting, am I not?
Covered, coated in
Loose hair, coal dust,
Black, black lung!
Black, black heart!
Have I committed this crime?
Won your accusations?
Nay!
Nay!
The righteous sleep soundly in their beds
And I am alongside them!
A wretched thing, yes!
Unearthly and unwanted,
Bound by hollow chains,
But absolved!
Filthy in form,
Cleanly in soul.

Ode to Sylvia

hold the coffin up to my ear.
vacant? no.
the rattle of an empty heart
echoes through its walls.
if i had to die alone
i should have learned
to live with myself.

A Confessionist Tale

I've never known who I am.
It was always just a guessing game.
Who do they want to see?
Who do I have to be
To live?
To pass?
To feel?

When I was with her it was simple.
I was hers,
No one else.
I didn't have to wonder.
I didn't have to guess.
I was hers.

Then I wasn't.

I was pulled back.
Personalities I formulated long ago
With detailed instructions
Rose from the shadows
With minds of their own
Clawing,
Killing
For recognition.

Who was I?
Someone cold.
Someone hollow.
A killer, maybe.
A writer.
A mind.
An empty decoration.

Pieces filtered in and out.
Some stayed for hours,
Some for years,
But always changing,
Exchanging one trait for another,
More appealing one.

Natural selection, I suppose,
But it's hard to trust yourself when your mind is a
Stranger.

I learned things,
Understood them.
I stopped lying so much because
People don't like liars,
And when the strings get tangled up so bad,
And you realize you've wrapped yourself
Like spiders' prey,
And the guilt sits in your stomach like a rock –
Or can I even feel? Is it guilt weighing me down
Or the realization that I've lost?

I was programmed to win,
Crafted carefully
Over a decade
And I failed - well,
It's time to make a change.
Another one.

When will it stop?
When we've perfected it, I suppose.
Perfected what?
Something kind? Intelligent? Creative? Cruel?
What thing have we been building?

A survivor.

Back to the drawing board, I suppose.

I've never known who I am.
It was always just a guessing game.

Wasteland

I can only assume you find my mind as I do –
A witless, overcrowded swampland –
Most unpleasant!
Riddled with muck and despair,
Crawling with strange little creatures –
Most unlovable!
And utterly unfamiliar in a civilized society,
To be sure,
Turmoil and filth live here.

Journey further?
Very well. Doubtless, as you carry on,
You shall, quite unfortunately,
Stumble upon my heart.
The ground shall rise and dry,
Shrivel before the merciless sun,
And crumble beneath its rays.
A cracked, bitter desert,
To be sure.
Inhospitable – nothing lives here long,
Or indeed, nothing here lives long.
Were you hoping for an oasis?
A stray, juicy cactus full of life blood?
A wasted prayer!
An antipathetic land
As far as life is concerned.

On we go?
The soul lies next on our venture.
What then?
Why, nothing.
And not nothing in the sense that I am

Unaware of a somethingness –
Nothing in the fact of nothingness –
Just emptiness.
Not pain, nor joy.
Not love, nor heartbreak –
No, nothing at all.

And on to the soul we go.

You'll know you've reached it when
The sun frosts over and freezes in its place
Deep beneath the horizon.
Ice and snow.
Beautiful, no?
Beautiful? No.
Only in the twisted sense of beauty
As a finely made gravestone –
Expertly crafted, to be sure –
But it sparks no joy,
No profound sense of wonder.
Numbness,
Cruelty,
These things dwell here.
Linger long,
Question the steady silence,
And the tundra takes.
It knows not the price it demands,
Only that it was never meant to cede an inch.

Leaving so soon?

Lost Myth of True Love

i don't know how to exist
without her
by my side.

whispers and prayers
bleed into the mossy soil
feeding her cenotaph.

i don't know
what she would say
if i told her what i've done.

when she calls me home
i'll ask her if it has been enough
to deserve her adoration,
to make her proud.

...

my love,
you have suffered greater than i
and rose to reverence,
but without you,
i am unbalanced
and adrift.

directionless,
i wander these moors,
trying to uphold your name
while every recollection of you
shatters me,
and every moment without you
is desolation.

Who will Jail the Jailor?

What would the jailor be
Without the jailed?
A rattler of empty keys?
No man beholden to his law?
It is not the order,
It is not the way.

A king must have his subjects,
A jailor must have his jailed.

Who, you ask?
Well there are always some.

Herd the masses,
Green paper pups nipping their heels,
And take your pick!

Her! She speaks too loudly
and too often.
Him! His dark skin
shall make a darker coffin.
Her! Beneath that scarf
her mind has softened.

Tread lightly
Lest he cage you too.

Is he just? Unlikely.
When he confronts
His small mill
Of existence,
He shall gaze
Into the mirror of veracity
And tremble.

I am, I am, I am

I am the keeper of keys.
I hear the songbirds scream,
Frozen in cages of stone,
And wonder what troubles them so.

I am the soldier of ice.
Not versed enough for command,
Nor brave enough for a savior,
I lay the frost where I am told,
And feel the flowers crack beneath my soles.

I am the watcher.
Hidden in my greenery,
The world is cold,
But I am free.

I am the caged songbird.
But no one sings for me,
They've clipped my wings,
So here I scream,
Among the forgotten,
Turned to stone.

Hate Yourself, Love Me Instead

who is it
you think i am?
you have clouded your mind with conceptions,
so tell them true.

do not preach your soul to me,
i neither envy nor desire it,
barely tolerate.

i am
stubborn and ungrateful,
do not think
pity can sway me,
pride would be a safer bet.

i will not
love you
for your dignitaries.

i am
an inescapable animal
bound only to the wild.
you are
too frail
to taste the blood on my tongue.

Honey

What is it you do to me? You
Rearrange the cynicism of my DNA,
Leave my heart open as prey,
Pray, tell me what is it you do to me?

How can the thought of you burn
Through my stomach like tender acid?
Setting parts of me aflame
I believed were frozen and tame,
What is it you do to me?

How can you
So swiftly
So effortlessly
Invade my heart
And conquer my mind?
What is it, great soldier, that you do to me?

How can I
Become so utterly devoted
After a few simple words
Drip from your mouth
Like sweet, southern
Honey?

Shit Happens

What happens when I have shared it all?
When you have soaked up
Every drop of my heart?
What happens when I grow tired?
Bored?
When the butterflies shrivel and sink
And I realize I am
Incapable of loving another?
What happens when you realize I am
Corrupt and volatile,
Living in the bygones and forgottens,
The what-ifs and maybe-some-days?

When I wake at night
And can't remember my own name
Or the shape of my mother's face
Or the feeling
Of adrenaline surging through my veins,
What makes you so sure
You will still occupy
An ounce of space
In my mind?

Two-Dimensional

sweet dreams of darkness
tremble before
her wrath.
death, my darling,
haunts the wake of our idolatry,
raising emerald paper
to the height of gods,
two-dimensional in nature
destined for depravity.

Government-Assigned Bottom Feeder

glass heart?

no. ice.

I am your creation.

I am your downfall.

haven't you heard?

C'est La Vie

Like most dreamers
I am selfish.
I have tried to undo the fabric of my DNA
Unsatisfied
With the destiny I saw woven there.
I have tried to rewrite my existence
With the simple finesse
Of turning over a blank page.
I have failed.

I will summon
My fleeting strength
And accept that
If I cannot outrun Death,
I must join her.

12
9
3
6

Disheartened and Desecrated

have you felt the cool touch of oblivion?
known the peace of heaven's black amnesia?
i heard the great oak cough
and knew my time had come.
i heard the white wind shiver
and knew our rule was done.
disheartened and desecrated,
the earth returns to her orderly chaos,
free from the conqueror's grasp.

Not Death but Annihilation

every brush of your hand
reveals to me
all the love
i possess
but can never
requite.

if i can't be satisfied
with simply existing
in your reality,
perhaps you'll still haunt me
in mine.

…

when i am extinguished
from this earth
will i cease to exist?
will you cherish
the memory i leave behind?
or am i but directionless stardust,
cyclical in nature
unbeholden to the world?

The More You Give Me

The more you give me
The more hollow I become.

I see darkness in you.
Inch by inch
I'll pull it from between your teeth.
Give me everything,
And watch me leave
A stranger.

I don't love you.
I'm not sure
I'd know it if I did.
As much as I like
The idea of a home,
Impermanence has always ruled me.

I can't remember my real name.
When I stare into the mirror,
Pick apart the bits
Of dead skin and peach fuzz,
I am left
A vessel,
Nothing more.

I will never be satisfied.
Not if the moon
Rose from the tides
To plant her shimmering kiss

Upon my head.
Not if you fell to your knees
And swore on every god you've ever known
That you would perish,
Rot in hell with me,
If I would just say those words.

But I can't.
I can't love you.

A Stream of Unconsciousness

I am a wild thing,
Impermanent in nature,
In all but nature.

Love me with such magnitude and fire
That you find yourself
Lost in me.

I know I've lost my mind,
But you have yet to taste
The bittersweet tragedy
Of my amnesia.

I will consume you,
Mind, body, and soul,
Until you are left
Bare and without restraint.

These are the ramblings of a madman.
These are the ramblings of a madman.

I write as if any moment
My mind will cease to exist
And this page will be left
Half-written,
Two-dimensional,
Incomplete
As I am.

Help Me Dig These Graves

You have to believe me,
I did it for the greater good.
Greater good?
I'm sorry.
I never earned it.
I never earned anything.

I can't do this on my own.
I feel the need to kill
But never want to die.
I'll dig two graves
To be safe.

Invasive and Unknowable

my own memories
don't seem real.

i am someone else
imprisoned in this body,
this mind,

rewritten in a life
that was never mine
to begin with.

Womanhood: Haikus

Heavy is my heart,
I feel so inadequate
In the wake of dreams.

Lover of Sappho,
She was a gift of the gods,
Woven in my mind.

Stifled at her birth,
Abandoned at womanhood,
So sweetly subdued.

To lay with the Lost,
Die among the Romantics,
Oh, fortunate me!

Keep me close, my dear,
I don't know how to exist
Outside of chaos.

Satisfy, Satiate, Sedate

You're going crazy, dear.
Well, I don't know how to do anything else.

I wish I could give you what you want.
It's a future I dream of
But can never possess.

I could never have a child
I'm terrified I wouldn't love it
If it wasn't like me,
And I'd hate it if it was.

I feel such relief when I cry.
It happens so rarely
I cherish it when it comes.

I can't tell what's real anymore.
Can't focus on a singular moment
My dreams seem infinitely more true
Than my own memories.

Who is it
Whose body have I inhabited?
Whose life have I commandeered?
Please let me go

I want to recognize my name
And the sound of my voice
And the feeling of my skin on yours,

But I can't.

It's just not mine.

I'm not sure

How much longer I can exist

A stranger to myself.

Break the Wheel

He did this to me.
He made me this way.
Corrupt and volatile.
A cold,
Unfeeling
Killer.

I didn't
Ask for this.
The only time I feel
Like a person is when I'm angry.
Luckily,
I'm almost always angry.

He ruined me.
I was kind,
Gifted,
Ambitious.
But he didn't know what he was doing.
I can't hate him for what he did,
But he changed me
And the hate lives on.
I can't hate him,
Not for that.
He made me.
I love him,
Because he's him.
I hate him.
Because so am I.

We Shall Meet in the Place Where There is No Darkness

It is a monotonous world
I am conditioned to
But one I struggle
To recognize.

Every day I grow less tethered
To this fixed perspective,
This finite reality.
I long for the overlapping,
Indifferent chaos
Of the crashing waves
And know that someday
I will leave this place
And return home
To the ocean
I seek.

Forgive Me for My Failing Health

At what point does this stop being déjà vu?
Every move I make
Is calculated, whittled down
To the bare essence of humanity:
Greed.

I don't crave you,
But I will consume you,
Like an overripe plum,
I won't enjoy you,
But I will take all of you,
And leave you nothing but your core.

I fear stability almost as much
As I fear change I cannot control.
Teach me how to be a person.
You are good
And I want to be good.

I don't want to burden you.
I am a creature
Of high risk,
But high reward.

I want to be good,
But I'm scared
If I was,
I would find myself

Unrecognizable.
My world
Is already a haze
And I can't lose me too.

All I've Ever Done is Hide

i burned my feet
and cut my hands,
it was my penance.

up here i am whole.
up here i am free.

i live in the clouds now.
he can't get to me now.
now, only the great oak trees
can see me smile.
and now,
they do.

Apocalypse

They're swarming me, darling,
Like rotting meat.
They're chasing me, darling,
Like crazed vultures.

I'm not dead, darling,
It's not my time.
Time.
My fiercest rival
And greatest benefactor.
Time.
Fleeting and indifferent,
A fine match
For my humbled soul.

She hasn't killed me yet, darling.
Why are they swarming me?
Tell them I'm alive.
Tell them
I'm done running.

The Devil Makes Three

I wanted to kill you.
Sometimes I still do.

I became
Uncontrollable,
Unfillable
Pit of rage.

If I could scream
Until my ears bled
And my lips shriveled up
And all the breath I had
Siphoned out of my cracked lungs,
I could die happy
Knowing I'd never
Have to hear your voice again.

On the Run

I found comfort
And happiness
For the briefest of moments,
I was, once more,
A person.

And then you came
To remind me
That the hand I was dealt
Is incapable of
Love.

The very word reverberates through
My hollow rib cage,
Slicing me to the bone,
Rendering me
Cold and distant,
On the run again.

Deport Me to the Promised Land

Sugar grass
And trees that weep in the wind
Like widows of the Lost –
This is the promised land.
Razor thin petals
And glass bulbs of fruit
Shatter against the ground –
This is the promised land.
Me, satisfied and soaring,
And you, pressing me to be
Sober and safe –
This is the promised land
And I am free.

The Invasion

In all these boxes
Of bits of ribbon,
The died-too-young,
And old memories,
There is not one framed picture of me.
These boxes safeguard a legacy
I don't belong to.
Why do I hoard them?
In every photograph
I look like I have been
Cut and pasted in
With too much glue
And too little heart.
This isn't my life.
I am a tourist.
I made my way into a few pictures,
But none worthy enough to frame,
None worthy enough
To justify the invasion
Of intimate moments
Reserved for family.

The Watcher

Two glowing red eyes
Beacon from the darkness.
Petrified,
I am frozen as I lie.
He knows all I have done.
Every sickness that has invaded
My consciousness,
Every moment of weakness,
Every dream of pain.

He is here to judge me,
Weigh my heart.
He is here to condemn me.

Then why did you not stop me?
Why did you watch me
Descend into monstrosity?
If you are
So omnipresent,
So all-knowing,
Why did you not intervene?

It wasn't his place.
He is not a meddler,
As I am.
He is the impartial,
Patient
Watcher.

He is condemned
To watch,
To know,
Without any power to impact.

Beautiful, is he not?
Elusive, am I not?

He is the glowing light
Of passion,
Restrained by darkness.

I am the darkness
That cages and stifles.

Forever at draw.

Unmercy

Violent.
Uncontrollable.
It stalks me in the dead of night,
Waiting for the opportune moment
To destroy me.

By all means, take it.
After all,
This isn't really my body,
I'm only borrowing it.

I am no more tethered to this vessel
Than I am to the fleeting thoughts
That stow away within the corners of my mind.

I am not tethered to this body,
And I hope the same is true for you,
On the off chance that
You are left unrecognizable
At the unmercy of a woman.

Do what you must
And I'll do the same.

Atlas Come Home

Have you ever
Locked yourself away
In such convincing narratives
And fantasies
That the abrupt realization
Of reality
Was an affront?

I was bombarded with silence.
I wish I could say I was.
She wasn't angry with me,
She knew that all I have done
I did to distract myself,
Because the great weight of her existence
Was too much to bear all at once.

The silence didn't bombard me,
She greeted me
Like an old, unforgotten friend.
A wayward child who strayed too far
Searching for purpose in the sporadic,
Overlapping noise
Of outside.
A cracked pillar
Who fled the heavy burden
To not have to
Witness the skies crumble
Before her own eyes.

She held me close,
Let me trace my fingers
Over her curves,
And let her weight
Sink back into me.

Atlas come home,
Atlas come home.

Fire Burn and Cauldron Bubble

The hunt never ends at the grave
And I cannot escape the fluidity
Of this slow,
Aching death.

Like squalling animals,
We settle into
Our cramped, lonely cages
Over time.

Inquisitive, but not intelligent,
Although we hold the capacity,
An educated mass would be an unruly one.
Best we are left sedated,
Culpable to their will.

We suffer,
Enough to cause pain,
Not enough to evoke a lasting urgency.

Some have realized
We are being slowly, deliberately boiled,
But those who scream before their time
Are quickly silenced
By the overlookers
Who carefully stoke the flame
And blame the fire on the match itself
And not the man who struck it.

Untitled

I am human.
Why does no one believe me?

You don't even believe yourself.

Help is coming, they said,
But I know a part of him reveled in it.
Recovery is coming, they said,
But how can I recover?

This is his crime,
So why do I bear the guilt?

Help is coming, they said.

What help
What help

I

Dead to Me

If you were to leave this plane tomorrow
Would I cry
Or be relieved?
That the great, imposing burden
Has been lifted from my aching chest.

You hurt me,
I adapted.
You changed me,
I killed you.

I grieved at your gravestone
Long before you were ever in the ground.

So, when the time comes
That your body is preened
And your casket carried out for all to see,
How will I weep?
When you have long been dead to me.

Homespun Destiny

I am comforted,
For I hold a deep, unwavering assurance
That our singularity is not confined
To the space between what is now
And what is to come.

I am shrouded in the knowing
That beyond the unknowable,
We will reunite, once more,
In the quiet devotion
Of our homespun destiny,
Unbounded at last.

Forevermore

Although I can never
Fully remedy the afflictions of your heart,
I find contentment in my venture to ease
Whatever aching I come across.

And although the idea
That, one day,
Another shall take my place
By your side
Is nigh unbearable,
I satisfy myself in making
Every moment
Unforgettable
So I may occupy your mind
Forevermore.

Home With You

could we run?
leave this hulking déjà vu
and flee to the forest?
i want to sink
into the soil
and be nourished
by the cooling moss
and healed
by your gentle touch.

my bones are burning
and my joints are stiff.
i feel trapped
in this repetition,
but you
are a glimpse
into life outside this cycle
of birth and rebirth,
of dying but not quite dead.

escape with me
to the land of old,
where ancient beings
loom above us and spread below.
i want to learn
how to plant roots
and cultivate a future
with you.

EMMA MATHEWS

ABOUT EMMA MATHEWS

Inspired by her school's Creative Writing Club and encouraged by her teachers, Emma Mathews has been writing since she was twelve years old (at the writing of this book she is sixteen). Her poetry has won regional and national awards from the Scholastic Art and Writing Awards—the nation's longest-running and most prestigious recognition program for creative teens in grades seven through twelve.

Not surprisingly, she has gone on to become the Vice President of her high school's writing club. In the near future Emma plans to write more poetry and delve into creating novels.

Emma lives with her family in northern California, and in her spare time enjoys baking, reading, and playing with her dog, Guinness!

Connect with Emma at www.AcheloisBooks.com

Made in the USA
Las Vegas, NV
16 September 2021

30351597R00049